The Urbana Free Library

To renew: call **217-367-4057**
or go to **urbanafreelibrary.org**
and select **My Account**

BE AN
ELECTRICIAN

Published in the United States of America by Cherry Lake Publishing
Ann Arbor, Michigan
www.cherrylakepublishing.com

Content Adviser: Seth Flavin, Electrical Tech Instructor, North Central Kansas Technical College, Beloit, KS
Reading Adviser: Marla Conn, MS, Ed., Literacy specialist, Read-Ability, Inc.

Photo Credits: Cover and page 1, ©thanatphoto/Shutterstock; page 5, ©Scott Alan Ritchie/Shutterstock; page 6, ©roman023/
iStockphoto.com; page 8, ©Robert Blouin/Shutterstock; page 11, ©Rawpixel.com/Shutterstock; page 12, ©fstop123/iStock-
photo.com; page 14, ©Phovoir/Shutterstock; page 16, ©Pormezz/Shutterstock; page 19, ©XiXinXing/Shutterstock; page 20,
©Etaphop photo/Shutterstock; page22, ©ALPA PROD/Shutterstock; page 25, ©Cineberg/Shutterstock; page 26, ©Minerva
Studio/Shutterstock; page 28, ©topten22photo/Shutterstock

Library of Congress Cataloging-in-Publication Data
Names: Mara, Wil, author.
Title: Be an electrician / by Wil Mara.
Description: Ann Arbor, Michigan : Cherry Lake Publishing, [2019] | Series:
 21st century skills library | Includes bibliographical references and
 index.
Identifiers: LCCN 2019003505| ISBN 9781534148253 (lib. bdg.) | ISBN
 9781534149687 (pdf) | ISBN 9781534151116 (pbk.) | ISBN 9781534152540
 (ebook)
Subjects: LCSH: Electrical engineering—Vocational guidance—Juvenile
 literature. | Electricians—Juvenile literature.
Classification: LCC TK159 .M365 2019 | DDC 621.319/24023—dc23
LC record available at https://lccn.loc.gov/2019003505

Cherry Lake Publishing would like to acknowledge the work of The Partnership for 21st Century Learning.
Please visit www.p21.org for more information.

Printed in the United States of America
Corporate Graphics

ABOUT THE AUTHOR

Wil Mara is the author of over 175 fiction and nonfiction books for children. He has written
many titles for Cherry Lake Publishing, including the popular *Global Citizens: Modern Media*
and *Citizen's Guide* series. More about his work can be found at www.wilmara.com.

TABLE OF CONTENTS

CHAPTER 1

The Electrician's Life

Michael Simmons is awoken from a deep sleep in the middle of the night. He's been a professional electrician for 10 years. He likes his job very much, but he likes a good night's sleep, too. He gets one most of the time. But not always. Electrical work is usually a nine-to-five profession when there aren't any emergencies. But sometimes there are nights like this.

Michael grabs his phone. The text message tells him that a **transformer** has blown in the next town over from his. It's one of the big units sitting near the top of a utility pole. Specifically, these are called distribution transformers. They are part of a larger system where electricity is generated at a

Damaged power lines, transformers, and other equipment need to be repaired promptly because they can be dangerous.

power plant and sent through a network of wires and cables to be used in homes and businesses. The transformer can be thought of as the last link in this chain before the power reaches its final destination.

Michael dresses quickly. His work clothes include a thick set of overalls and a pair of leather shoes with rubber soles. The rubber soles are particularly important because electrical **current** cannot travel through them. Once Michael gets to

Line workers cannot be afraid of heights. They spend a lot of time high above the ground in crane buckets.

the job **site**, he will put on other safety items as well. These include a hard hat, a pair of safety glasses, and insulated gloves. His clothing also has to have an appropriate **arc rating** to ensure that it has a high resistance to flame. In the event of an electrical accident, the arc-rated clothing will protect Michael from the high temperatures and flames of an electrical arc flash.

Michael gets into his truck and heads toward the blown transformer. He works for a local utility company as a line repairer. This means he maintains the high-voltage power lines and other equipment that deliver electricity to homes and businesses.

Other electricians work on the wiring in homes or businesses. But Michael likes that he gets to work outdoors. He also likes knowing that his work can help many people all at once. The downside is that he sometimes has to answer emergency calls like this one.

Michael gets to the site and finds other service people already there. Bright lights are shining up at the blown transformer. It has big black marks along its sides. This means it caught fire at some point. Michael has dealt with transformer problems before. He's already sure this one can't be fixed. It will need to be replaced. Fortunately, someone has already brought a new transformer to the site. This means the many homes and businesses that are currently without power will be up and running again fairly soon.

Michael climbs into the bucket of a service truck, and a big crane unfolds to lift him up. All his tools are with him in the bucket. Among them is a device called a hot stick. This long

A hot stick allows a line worker to flip switches, attach wires, and more.

pole is made of fiberglass, so electricity cannot travel through it. Michael can attach different tools to the end of the stick. Then he can use it to work on the live electrical equipment on the power line without getting shocked.

Michael drills new holes into the pole and uses them to attach new mounting equipment. Then the new transformer is lifted up by a second crane. Michael guides it into place and attaches it to the mounting plates he installed. The dead transformer is detached and lowered down. The whole job takes a few hours. By the time Michael is driving back home, the sun is beginning to rise. And he still has a full day of his usual work ahead! But Michael doesn't mind. All around him, thousands of people are now very happy that their lights, refrigerators, computers, and televisions are working again.

21st Century Content

On average, roughly 670,000 electricians are employed in the United States each year. The states that employ the most are listed here:

California—63,000
Texas—60,000
New York—42,000
Florida—37,000
Ohio—24,000

How to Become an Electrician

Becoming an electrician does not require a college degree. But this doesn't mean electricians don't need any education at all. In fact, quite the opposite is true. It takes a lot of skill and knowledge to solve issues with electrical systems. Electrical work also poses certain dangers that are increased without proper training.

The first step toward becoming an electrician is to get a high school diploma or the equivalent. While high schools do not generally offer specific training in the electrical field, they still cover subjects that every future electrician should study carefully. Mathematics, for example, is a very important topic

Studying electronics in school is a great way to prepare for a career as an electrician.

Good communication skills will come in handy for any electrician, especially those who work face-to-face with customers.

for an electrician. Everything from basic addition and subtraction to algebra and trigonometry will play a role in an electrician's day-to-day work. Measuring the length of wiring or figuring out the size of a circuit, for example, will be part of the job. Science classes will also come in handy. A typical high school physics class will introduce some of the fundamentals of electricity. Even English classes can be very important for electricians. Good reading and writing skills are essential for communication. This is especially useful for electricians who run their own business. They will need to be able to communicate with clients, vendors, and many other people both in writing and face-to-face.

Life and Career Skills

There are many different career paths one can take within the field of electrical work. The most common is a residential electrician. This is the person who comes to someone's home to fix problems or install new wiring. Residential electricians must be comfortable meeting new people all the time and communicating with their customers.

Commercial electricians specialize in electrical systems for offices, stores, and other locations that are not residential. Sometimes these workers are employed directly by a single business to maintain that business's electrical system full-time. In other situations, they work for electrical companies and complete jobs for many different businesses.

Industrial electricians are somewhat like commercial electricians. However, they work on electrical systems in places such as factories and utility plants. This requires them to have specific knowledge of the high-powered systems these facilities rely on.

A mentor is able to provide guidance and advice as student electricians work on their first real jobs.

After high school, future electricians should consider attending some sort of trade or vocational school that has specific courses in electrical training. Some community colleges offer these kinds of classes. Students will learn about electrical theory, national electrical **codes**, and electrical system design. They will also be taught how to read **blueprints** and use a variety of specialized tools.

Students in trade or vocational programs do more than read books and take tests. There is a great deal of hands-on training. This provides students with the opportunity to develop the technical skills they will use on the job every day. The average time to complete a program in these schools can be anywhere from six months to a year. Some schools also offer the option to earn an associate's degree in two years.

Once a student finishes with formal schooling, the next step is to begin learning skills firsthand on the job. This is generally done through an **apprenticeship**. An apprenticeship requires the student to accompany a professional electrician in real-life work situations. The experienced professional acts as a mentor and guide, ensuring that the apprentice learns the trade with minimal risk to themselves or others. An apprenticeship usually begins with an application process. This process is handled through the state's labor board. A basic skills test is sometimes required, plus some physical testing, a personal interview, and usually even a drug test.

Once all of these requirements have been completed, an apprentice can begin working. Apprentices are exposed to every part of the electrician's trade, such as installation, repair,

An electrician might route wires through metal tubes called conduits to install a new electrical outlet.

and maintenance of wiring, fixtures, and other aspects of electrical systems. They will also learn how to assure that systems meet local code requirements. The professionals overseeing their apprentices will show them how to perform tests on systems using specialized testing equipment.

The average apprenticeship lasts about four years, but some can go as long as five or six years. Afterward, a successful apprentice is ready to become a **licensed** professional. To qualify for a license, one usually has to reach certain levels of both education and on-the-job experience. These requirements vary from state to state. For example, one state may require a minimum of 500 hours of classroom instruction plus 5,000 hours of training in real work situations. Another might only require 4,000 hours of on-the-job experience.

Once an apprentice meets the local requirements and obtains a license, he or she becomes a professional electrician. From there, higher levels of qualification can be achieved through work experience. The two most common are **journeyman** and **master**. Master is the highest recognized level in the electrician's trade. Becoming a master electrician requires holding a journeyman's license for at least two years, plus around 12,000 hours of work experience under the supervision of someone who has already attained master status. Those who hope to become master electricians must also pass an exam given by their home state.

CHAPTER 3

The Ins and Outs of Being an Electrician

As with any other profession, being an electrician has its good days and its bad days. The work can be very rewarding, but it can also pose some serious challenges.

On the downside, there are the hours. Most electricians get to follow a nine-to-five schedule—but not always. The story at the beginning of this book shows just how unpredictable the job can be. Emergencies in the middle of the night are not all that uncommon. An electrician may also have to travel long distances to a job site. If the electrician lives in a heavily populated area with a lot of traffic, these trips could take quite a while. Time spent on the road can add up quickly.

Installing light fixtures in the ceiling is just one of an electrician's many responsibilities when working on a new home.

A device called a multimeter allows an electrician to measure the amount of electricity that flows through an outlet.

Working as an electrician is a very physical profession. Electricians have to lift and carry heavy objects. They work with heavy tools and other equipment. Sometimes they have to operate within cramped spaces. Some days will require long periods of standing or kneeling. This can take a toll on an electrician's body, especially as he or she gets older.

There are also safety risks any time an electrician goes to work. The most obvious danger is that of electrical shock. A quick, low-voltage shock will do little more than put a scare into someone. But greater amounts of electricity can cause serious injury. The good news is there are many safety precautions an electrician can take on the job. This includes wearing safety gear, using the correct tools, staying aware of nearby energized equipment at all times, and de-energizing electrical equipment when it isn't being used.

On the upside, pursuing a career as an electrician can lead to a secure, well-paying job. Qualified electricians usually do not have any trouble finding steady work. This is especially true in the more populated areas of the country, where the high number of homes and other buildings means plenty of

Electricians often find themselves squeezing into tight spaces.

electrical needs. There are about 670,000 electricians working in the United States, and the rate of job growth is around 10 percent per year.

The pay is fairly good, too. The average electrician earns about $54,000 per year. That breaks down to about $26 per hour. Those who stick with the profession will earn better money over time. At the top of the scale, some electricians earn $90,000 to $100,000 per year. In many cases, an electrician will also have the opportunity to work overtime, which can mean up to double their normal pay. The trade-off with overtime is that it requires working weeknights, weekends, or even holidays.

Many electricians enjoy the benefits that come with being a member of a **union**. A union negotiates with employers to seek more pay and other important benefits, such as a pension plan or health insurance, on behalf of its members.

21st Century Content

An electrical contractor is not the same as an electrician. An electrician is someone who performs actual electrical work. An electrical contractor is a person or business who employs electricians.

When a construction company is building a new home, it typically hires other companies to do all the different types of work. This includes hiring carpentry, plumbing, and electrical companies. These smaller companies then offer contracts to workers. The bulk of electrical jobs in the United States—about two out of every three—come from electrical contractors or similar companies.

CHAPTER 4

Laws and Regulations

All electricians are required to follow laws and regulations. These rules exist not only for the safety of everyone involved— including the electricians, their co-workers, and their employers—but also to ensure that they produce the best-quality work possible.

First and foremost, an electrician must be licensed in order to work. Each state has its own licensing requirements. However, all of them follow a series of strict standards. And not all electrical licenses are the same—there are different licenses for different electrical specialties. Some licenses have restrictions as to where within a state an electrician is permitted to work. A certified electrician can work

Electricians have to pay careful attention to their work to ensure it meets the standards of the National Electrical Code.

anywhere within the state where their license has been issued. A registered electrician, however, can only work in a specific area.

Obtaining an electrician's license is not simply a matter of filling out forms and sending in a check. In most cases, the electrician will need to pass an exam. Much of the exam will concern the National Electrical Code—a set of guidelines specifically covering the installation of wiring and the operation of specialized tools and other equipment within the United States. Passing the licensing exam proves that the

Just like workers in many other jobs, electricians sometimes have to complete paperwork.

electrician has attained a certain level of knowledge and experience.

Life and Career Skills

Anyone thinking about starting their own electrical firm, whether as a for-hire electrician or a contractor, should take the time to learn basic aspects of business. Among the most important business skills are cost estimation, customer relations, and project management.

Cost estimations need to be precise. Mistakes in this area can cost huge amounts of money. Nothing will upset a customer faster than finding out they have to spend more money than they were originally told.

Customer relations are important for repeat business. Also, happy customers are more likely to recommend an electrician to their friends and neighbors. On the other hand, an unhappy customer might leave a negative review online, making it harder for the electrician to find new work.

Project management is all about keeping everything running smoothly. A business owner has to keep track of schedules, costs, and every other aspect of each project. This can be challenging some days because there are so many moving parts to running a business.

Customers can rest assured that a licensed and bonded electrician will be skilled and dependable.

It is illegal for an unlicensed electrician to work, though this still happens from time to time. The risks in such a situation are numerous. First, an unlicensed electrician probably cannot promise the same quality of work as a licensed one. Second, anyone who knowingly hires an unlicensed electrician is likely to be in violation of state law.

Being **bonded** is just as important as being licensed. Put simply, a bond is a type of insurance policy that covers any damage caused by an electrician while on the job. No matter how many safety precautions an electrician takes, there is still always a chance that something can go wrong. For example, faulty electrical wiring can easily cause a fire. This could burn a house to the ground. A bond covers the cost of any damage caused by this type of error, whether or not it is the electrician's fault. Without a bond, the employer can end up with no way to pay for the damage. In such cases, it is not unusual for the electrician to end up being sued.

There are requirements for becoming bonded. Even though these requirements vary from state to state, a few general qualifications will always apply. The electrician has to be licensed, which ensures a certain level of experience and education. The amount of bond that is issued will depend in part on the electrician's annual income. Finally, electricians with fewer accidents in their past will have an easier time getting a bond. The more incidents an electrician has, the less likely it is that a company will want to insure them. A bond will also be more difficult to obtain if the electrician has a criminal history.

Think About It

People have been using electricity, in one form or another, since at least as far back as 600 BCE. That's when ancient Greeks realized they could produce static electricity by rubbing pieces of fur together. But electricity as we know and use it today wasn't really developed until the early 1800s. In 1831, inventor Michael Faraday built the first dynamo. This device generated electricity when a metal disk was turned within a magnetic field. In the years ahead, significant improvements were made on his idea, resulting in the first reliable **generators**. What do you suppose people used these early generators for? And what kinds of dangers do you think they posed?

There is a lot of information online about the different careers you could pursue in the electrical industry. Which one do you feel would be right for you, and why? Explain your choice. Which parts of the electrician's lifestyle do you think you'd like the most? What about the least?

Find Out More

BOOKS

Labrecque, Ellen. *Electrician*. Ann Arbor, MI: Cherry Lake Publishing, 2017.

Teitelbaum, Michael. *Electrician*. Ann Arbor, MI: Cherry Lake Publishing, 2016.

WEBSITES

EIA Energy Kids—Science of Electricity Basics
www.eia.gov/kids/energy.php?page=electricity_science-basics
Find out more about how electricity works at this website from the U.S. Energy
Information Administration.

**U.S. Bureau of Labor Statistics—Occupational Outlook Handbook:
Electricians**
https://www.bls.gov/ooh/construction-and-extraction/electricians.htm
Learn how to become an electrician and more about the profession at this
government site.

GLOSSARY

apprenticeship (uh-PREN-tis-ship) an arrangement where someone learns a skill by working with an expert on the job

arc rating (ARK RAY-ting) a measurement of the amount of energy a fabric can absorb before the person wearing it will become burned

blueprints (BLOO-printz) drawings that illustrate how a structure needs to be built

bonded (BAHND-id) having an insurance policy that covers damages caused by a worker while on the job

codes (KOHDZ) rules that determine the correct design and installation of an electrical system

current (KUR-rent) the flow of an electrical charge

generators (JEN-uh-ray-turz) mechanical devices that produce electricity

journeyman (JUR-nee-man) an electrician who has more experience, knowledge, and skill than an apprentice, but not as much as a master

licensed (LYE-suhnsd) given official certification to perform a job

master (MAS-tur) the highest recognized level of a professional electrician in terms of experience, knowledge, and skill

site (SITE) location of a job

transformer (trans-FOR-mer) a device that converts electrical energy into a different form

union (YOON-yuhn) an organization that protects the interests of a certain type of worker, such as an electrician

INDEX